In the Garden

Words by Eugene Booth

Pictures by Derek Collard

EAU CLAIRE DISTRICT LIBRARY

RAINTREE CHILDRENS BOOKS
Milwaukee • Toronto • Melbourne • London

Copyright © 1977, Macdonald-Raintree, Inc.

Library of Congress Number: 77-7628

   2 3 4 5 6 7 8 9 0 81 80 79 78

Printed and bound in the United States of America.

Library of Congress Cataloging in Publication Data

Booth, Eugene, 1940 —
   In the garden.

   (A Raintree spotlight book)
   SUMMARY: Uses a garden setting to stimulate such pre-
reading activities as counting, noting visual differences,
and making up a story.
[1.   Gardens]   I.   Collard, Derek.   II.   Title.
PZ7.B6467Il   [E]   77-7628
ISBN 0-8393-0115-4 lib. bdg.

In the Garden

This family is outside in the yard.
Which people are playing?
Which ones are working?

What might happen to these people?
Make up a story to go with the picture.
Turn the page and see what happens next.

Is this what you thought would happen?
What must each person do now?

How many animals can you find
in the picture? What has happened
to them in the story?

1
2
3
4

Four boots, three pots, two cans,
one rake. If you add them all —
how many will it make?

This picture is full of things in threes.
How many groups of three can you find?

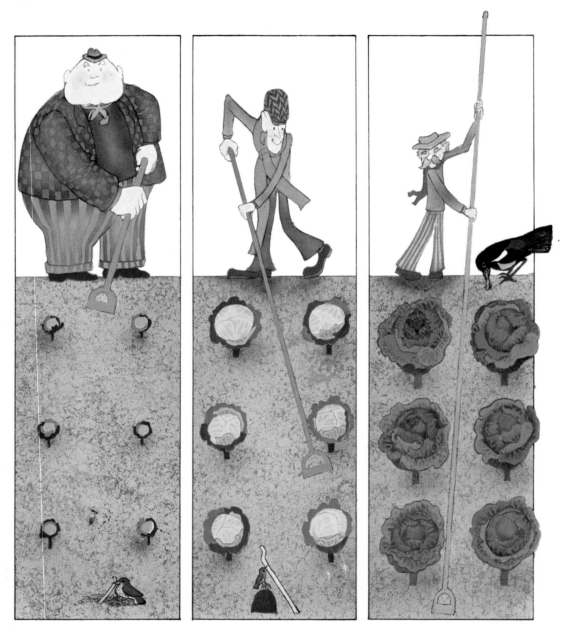

How many things can you find
that are three different sizes?
Which is the biggest thing in each group?

Which picture shows the inside of the cabbage? Which pictures show the outside? How many bugs and worms can you find?

This garden is full of color.
What colors do you see?
Can you count the red things?
The blue things? The yellow things?

What is each person in the picture doing?
Which things do you like to do?
Make up a story to go with this picture.

13

Look at the shapes below. Can you find the same shapes in this picture?

△ ○ ▭ ▢

14

Here is a story without words. Can you
tell the story from the pictures? What do
you think will happen next?

Did your story turn out this way?
How was your story different?
What might happen now?

The bee, the bird, and the spider are lost.
Can you help each one find its home?
Trace along each path.

Do you know the names of these fruits and vegetables? Which ones have you tasted? Which ones do you like?

Each of these shapes goes with something on the other page. Can you find where each shape fits?

Can you name the things in this picture?
There are four things in each group.
How are they alike?
How are they different?

20

What is wrong in this picture?
See if you can find all the mistakes.